CW00460432

Henry Marsh is a poet at the height of his powers. This new collection of poems, the latest in the torrent of creativity that has inspired his writing over the last few years, contains some of his finest work to date. For its gravity, its understanding, and its sheer beauty, *A Voyage to Babylon*, must surely take its place amongst the very best achievements of any contemporary poet writing in English.

Once again history provides the inspiration for the major sequence in this volume. Scottish history, in which Henry Marsh has immersed himself with such passion and enthusiasm, is no picnic. In these poems we find ourselves in the turbulent years of the seventeenth century when Scotland was racked by religious strife and dynastic argument. It is sometimes difficult, from our twenty-first century perspective, to understand why people were so exercised over these matters. In this collection Henry Marsh puts us in the very shoes of those involved and helps us to understand what it was to live in that blood stained and dramatic era. The result is an extraordinarily affecting poetic journey, as moving as it is enlightening.

But this book is not a history lesson. It is a lovely work of art in which language is used with remarkable effect. There is not a surplus word; there is not an image that could be bettered; there is no respect in which the dignity and sympathy that infuses these poems could be improved upon. And at the end, after reading the later, non-historical poems included as a second course to this feast, the reader is left with the sense of having been in the company of a wise and generous soul. And that, I think, is poetry's greatest gift.

Alexander McCall Smith

Henry Marsh was born in Broughty Ferry and now lives in Midlothian. He began writing on the death of a friend, a Gaelic Bard, Donald MacDonald of South Lochboisdale. His first collection of poems, *A First Sighting*, was published in 2005. Three other collections have followed, *A Turbulent Wake*, 2007, *The Guidman's Daughter*, 2009 and *The Hammer and the Fire* in 2011. In August 2008, he read at the Edinburgh International Book Festival. He has worked in collaboration with the Australian artist Kym Needle to produce *A Trail of Dreaming*, 2009, *Wayfarers*, 2011 and *Painted Trees*, 2012, paintings and poems that reflect Aboriginal themes.

Cover drawing by Kym Needle after Rembrandt's
The Storm on the Sea of Galilee.

A Voyage to Babylon

Henry Marsh
2013

For Katherine and Lucy

Also by Henry Marsh

A First Sighting, ISBN 978 0 9514470 1 7
first published in Great Britain in 2005 by Maclean Dubois,
Hillend House, Hillend, Edinburgh EH10 7DX

A Turbulent Wake, ISBN 978 0 9514470 4 8
first published in Great Britain in 2007 by Maclean Dubois.

A Trail of Dreaming, ISBN 13 978 0 9561141 0 5
in collaboration with the artist, Kym Needle,
published 2009 by the Open Eye Gallery,
34 Abercromby Place, Edinburgh EH3 6QE

The Guidman's Daughter, ISBN 978 0951 447062
first published 2009 by Maclean Dubois
distributed by Birlinn.

The Hammer and the Fire, ISBN 978 09565278 2 0
first published 2011 by Maclean Dubois
distributed by Birlinn

Painted Trees, ISBN 978 0 9561141 1 2
in collaboration with the artist, Kym Needle,
published 2012 by the Open Eye Gallery
34 Abercromby Place, Edinburgh EH3 6QE

Printed by InkSpotz 0131 553 6036
Design by Cate Stewart
Distributed by Birlinn Ltd
Copyright by Henry Marsh 2013

ISBN 978 0 9565278 4 4

Acknowledgements

I am much indebted to Professor Chrys Whatley and to George Harris who very kindly looked over the Introduction and prevented me from going too far astray in the thicket of 17th century Scottish history.

Peter Gilmour, as ever, was helpful with his suggestions about the poetry and its selection.

Little of the Covenanting material would have been accessible to me without the fascinating resources revealed in Robert Wodrow's, *The History of the Sufferings of the Church of Scotland from the Restoration to the Revolution*, published in two volumes, 1721-1722. I was able to download this book at the push of a button from Princeton University and for that facility I'm hugely grateful.

I must also thank Kym Needle for his time and skill in producing the cover image and his patience in responding to yet another of my strange requests. We selected one of half a dozen pieces he produced.

However, my greatest debt, once again, is to Professor Alexander McCall Smith and his team, who with good humour and unfailing efficiency, have facilitated the project. Thank you.

A Voyage to Babylon

A Voyage to Babylon

Introduction

The origins of this sequence of poems on the Covenanters lie in a visit to Dunnottar Castle and my re-visiting Sir Walter Scott's *Old Mortality*. More immediately, there are said to be Covenanters buried in our local Churchyard – casualties from Rullion Green – and it was a woman from our village who tended the corpse of George Renwick, 'Minister of the Moors', after his execution in the Grassmarket in Edinburgh in 1688.

I have derived the basic events in the sequence from Robert Wodrow's *The History of the Sufferings of the Church of Scotland from the Restoration to the Revolution*, published in two volumes, 1721-1722. I'm not in a position to question the slant of what he records but he was one of the first historians to use public records, manuscripts and personal accounts.

From *The Covenanters' Index* I discovered a list of the passengers on the 'Henry and Francis', the ship that transported the prisoners who survived Dunnottar to the American colonies. I chose a few names at random and was able to trace the movements of John Fraser through his exile and settlement in Connecticut – where he became a licensed preacher – until he and his wife returned to Scotland following the Glorious Revolution. To my surprise, I discovered that for a few years, he was the minister of Glencorse Kirk – just two or three miles from where I live.

However, although I have used the broad events of this period of his life, my account of him, and of all the other characters that nod in and out, is entirely fictional. In him, I wanted to explore not a fanatic but, nevertheless, a man of faith, a good man, and to think how he might have been changed by his remarkable experiences. James Forsyth, whose plight begins the story, I saw as someone swept up in events not wholly out of conviction but largely because of a moment of stubborn independence for which he and his family paid a terrible price. It also seemed to me important to include a deist, however briefly, a young man travelling as a passenger to America in search of intellectual and political freedom, someone grounded in Descartes and Spinoza and very much in touch with the rise of science associated, above all, with Newton, Thomas Hooke and the Royal Society. The contrast between religious fundamentalism and the incipient scientific spirit could hardly be more stark.

That places involved in 'The Killing Times' are just nearby, served to enhance my growing awareness of the immediacy of the past and fuelled my impulse to try, in however small a way, to approach it through my own writing. You catch, at moments, how frighteningly close history is.

• • •

In 1637 the attempts of Charles I to impose an English-style liturgy on the people of Scotland – devised by the Scottish bishops – led to riots in Edinburgh, popularly associated with the legendary Jenny Geddes allegedly throwing a stool at the minister's head in St Giles' following the introduction of the Anglican Book of Common Prayer – the 'English' Prayer Book. This incident is sometimes said to have sparked the Wars of the Three Kingdoms.

Scots dissent became focussed in the National Covenant, a document which an Edinburgh Lawyer, John Johnston of Wariston, helped draw up. On Wednesday, 28th February 1638 noblemen and barons signed it in Greyfriars' Kirkyard – some in their own blood. Wariston described the event as, 'that glorious marriage day of the Kingdome with God.' Over the following two days it was signed by many of the ministers and people of Edinburgh.

A previous National Covenant – the King's Confession or National Covenant – had been drawn up by John Craig in 1581 in response to efforts of the Roman Catholics to regain power in Scotland. It was based on the 1560 Scots Confession which had confirmed the Reformation in Scotland.

But though the 1637 Covenant sought to return to the form of religion that had existed in 1580, rejecting all subsequent changes, it also professed loyalty to the King. Copies of the document can still be found in Edinburgh, in St Giles' Cathedral and in Greyfriars' Kirk.

Unfolding events led to the raising of a Covenanting army to resist the religious reforms of Charles I and as a consequence of the Covenanters' victory at the battle of Newburn, in the second Bishops' War (1640), Scottish commissioners in London, supported by the London Puritans, negotiated the Treaty of London (1641) whereby the General Assembly's banishing of Episcopacy in Scotland was ratified. A grander aim that Presbyterianism should be adopted throughout the three kingdoms – to include England and Ireland – was dropped.

Charles' urgent attempts to raise money to pay the Scots' expenses for these wars put him in conflict with the Long Parliament at Westminster which ultimately led to the English Civil War, part of the Wars of the Three Kingdoms.

In 1643 the beleaguered English Parliament sought the aid of Scottish Covenanting armies. From this, emerged The Solemn League and Covenant, an agreement which the Scottish Presbyterians regarded as a religious covenant, another opportunity to further their aim to establish their reformed religion in England and Ireland. On the other hand, the English Parliamentarians saw it as a military treaty. Subsequently, the Scots' intention provoked dissent amongst the English Parliamentarians and some refused to take the prescribed oath. However, the urgency of defeating the Royalist forces held the league together and the Scots fought alongside the Parliamentarians, notably, at Marston Moor where Cromwell's cavalry proved, in the end, decisive (1644). Subsequent involvement of Covenanters in England was characterised by splits, shifting alliances and, eventually, in Scotland, battle between covenanting factions.

Episcopalians and Roman Catholics were bitterly opposed to the religious settlement in Scotland and between 1644 and 1645 civil war broke out. The Scottish Royalist army, led by James Graham, 1st Marquis of Montrose, augmented by Irish and Highland troops, won a series of victories which were finally reversed at the Battle of Philiphaugh, near Selkirk. In this action, the cry of the ministers amongst the Covenanting soldiers in battle was said to have been, 'Jesus and no quarter.' Prisoners and camp followers – women and children – were slaughtered.

On the face of it, the running paradox of this bitter strife was that neither side could conceive that religious freedom meant anything other than the triumph of one ideology over another. In reality, motives and aims were complex. Scott, in *Old Mortality*, represents a spectrum of attitudes engaged on both sides from the reasonable to the fanatical. And you can imagine that many were simply caught up in events and, doubtless, at times, choices were made on the grounds of expediency.

In England, after Marston Moor and the conclusion of the First English Civil War, neither the Independents of the New Model Army, nor the alliance of English and Scottish Presbyterians, nor the remaining Royalists were powerful enough to take the upper hand. The Presbyterians came to believe that their security lay in allying themselves with the remaining Royalists and an attempt was made to disband the New Model Army – Cromwell and the Army were now the common enemy. The Second English Civil War was engendered.

It ended at the Battle of Preston and victory for the Army. Subsequently, Charles I was tried and executed on 30th January 1649.

However, loyalty to the House of Stuart was deeply rooted in Scotland and the Scots persuaded the exiled Prince of Wales – later to become Charles II – to sign the Treaty of Breda in which he swore to honour the Solemn League and Covenant. This alliance again set the Covenanters at odds with the English Parliament. Consequently in 1650, Cromwell invaded Scotland.

Under Cromwell's occupation Scotland was forced into union with England and the Kirk lost all its civil power. Royalist uprisings occurred from time to time – Cromwell laid siege to Dunnottar Castle in 1651-52 – then on his death in 1658, his commander in Scotland, General Monck, calculated that the best interests of the kingdoms would be served by the restoration of the Stuarts. They were restored to power in 1660.

It is easy to skip through names of battles but the estimated numbers of Scottish casualties resulting from the Wars of the Three Kingdoms give pause for thought. It has been said that battlefield casualties were probably around 28,000. However, in those times, more soldiers died of the diseases they suffered than in actual combat. They also carried their diseases into the general population. So that in addition to the estimated 15,000 civilians who died as a direct result of war, probably 30,000 died of plague. And perhaps 20,000 Scottish troops died on English and Irish battlefields. The total population of Scotland at the time was probably around 1,000,000.

To get some perspective on these figures, perhaps 9% of the population of Scotland died directly or indirectly as a consequence of these wars, 3.7% of the population of England and a staggering 41% of the population of Ireland.

This period is one of the darkest in Scottish history. And if sectarianism is still manifest in contemporary Scotland, it is worth remembering that these terrible events occurred, roughly, only twelve generations back. Attitudes forged in suffering tend to evolve into myth which generates its own, autonomous power.

Once safely in power, in 1662 Charles II renounced the covenants and all those holding public office were required to abjure their oaths. Episcopacy was restored. The Covenanters were driven to hold their conventicles – their Presbyterian services – in secret and attendance at such meetings became a capital offence. Indeed, it was said that to be seen carrying a copy of the Geneva Bible could result in execution.

Rebellion simmered, and in 1666 a rag-tag, exhausted Covenanting army – some of them armed only with pitchforks – was routed at Rullion Green in the Pentland Hills near Edinburgh. In the defence of Edinburgh, the government forces were lead by Tam Dalziel – Bluidy Tam, the Muscovite de'il – an ancestor of Tam Dalziel, the former Labour MP. Nearly 1,200 hundred prisoners were taken and held in the churchyard of Greyfriars' Kirk. According to Presbyterian sources they suffered great cruelties – torture, brandings and executions. Those who survived were transported to the American colonies.

In an attempt to quell unrest in the South West the government resorted to using 6,000 Highland troops – the 'Highland Host' – and this 'occupation' came to be associated with many atrocities. Government troops were led by 'Bluidy Clavers' – John Graham of Claverhouse, Viscount Dundee. Some accounts suggest that executions were carried out on the spot without resort to trial. But whatever the reputation of Claverhouse amongst his enemies, it is worthy of note that he married into a prominent Covenanting family.

In 1679 the Covenanters had a remarkable victory over the forces of Claverhouse at Drumclog, near Glasgow. Subsequently, however, their effectiveness was severely compromised by in-fighting and the intransigence of the fanatics. They were swept away at the Battle of Bothwell Brig.

Opposition then found a focus in the Sanquar Declaration (1680) which more or less established a radical underground movement – the Cameronians. But their activities served to provoke even greater Government extremities. It was Wodrow who later designated this period of rebellion as 'The Killing Times'.

Then in 1685 information reached the Privy Council in Edinburgh that the Covenanting Duke of Argyle was sailing from exile in Holland to Orkney – Militia were mobilised and recusants swept up in the South West and marched to Edinburgh. Argyle's father had been executed in Edinburgh in 1661 and his son was to share the same fate in 1685. The trail to incarceration in Dunnottar Castle and transportation to America had begun.

God bless King James VII
By Lochmaben, May 1685

No canting enthusiast. But he'd seen
the harassing of the country. His friend,
John Hunter, had been shot at Corehead.
So it sticks in his throat. 'I wish
the King well. May all spiritual blessings
fall upon him.' Claverhouse smiles –
at least, the downturned mouth
twitches. His face is drawn, hollow-eyed,
'Forsyth, think on it. I require you
to bless our King – no more, no
less. I'll none of your damned whig
prevarications.' Silence. Clavers
waves him away.

Locked in a cellar. His hands tremble.
More pride than integrity?
That cool appraisal – the raised chin,
the half-closed eyes – that challenge,
the arrogance he'd risen to. Like stags
on a moss. And Lizzie with child.
Hour on hour, round and round,
re-living his rashness. Then he hears
the Life Guards' clattering passage –
and time, like a door, is a little ajar.
Clavers has departed. But he's dragged
into a twilit courtyard. Shivering,
he awaits his moment.

By the byre door an old man
is standing in prayer. He holds
a Bible to his chest. Then a file of prisoners
is led into the yard – a picket
stands guard and they settle as they can
till dawn. Light and birdsong
have never been so precious.
Racked by every stir - but militiamen
march them north. Swallows flicker
along Annan Water. As they pass
by Moffat, a pair of Ravens rise
from an oak tree – three eyeless
corpses swing.

The Fiery Cross
May 11th, 1685

Raw, from the east, an unseasonable wind.
New leaves tear and flutter,
sticks crack from old limbs.
Women and children stare from their doors
and wonder, feel chill in their bellies.

The Militia are raised – sixteen to sixty.
For Argyle is sailing for Orkney
and the Privy Council in a stir.
Recusants are harried like stray dogs,
the captives hard-driven to Edinburgh.

They watch fathers and sons – the butcher,
the baker, the candle-stick maker
and lairds on fine horses. Slowly
they pass. Their dust, their jingle and murmur
are swallowed in the whoom of the storm.

Somewhere a child is crying. They return
to their wintry Spring, step
into yesterday's lives like garments
that no longer quite fit. And white,
so white, the gean flowers falling.

The Tolbooth, Burntisland
May 19th, 1685

In two strait rooms
they sweated. Crushed in that throng,
some panicked, flailed and kicked
for air at the barred windows.
For the love of God, water.
And Mr Gilchrist, so strong
in the Word, a passion that rung
the very skies above the moors,
dumb, drooped like a dead bird,
and the piss trickling down his legs.

Over a short night
they'd ferried them from Leith.
He remembers a blue morning,
gulls limber and free
loud above the herring boats.
Home from home, crows
sulked on the corbie-stepped gables
and the weather cock scanned
the golden south over the sigh
and wash of a lazy tide.

Then sheep and goats – a day
of interrogations. But still he would
not swear. Though he knew
fine well the trade
in atrocities – how Ministers,

in victory, had clamoured, 'Jesus –
and no quarter.' And prisoners,
women and children, slaughtered.
'For God's high purposes
are beyond all law and decency.'

He'd looked at the straggling file –
men and women, old
and young, fleet and lame –
and could not compromise:
a king's duty is to serve his people.
Now, in a new dawn, a breeze
through the night's rank breath
and out of its flowing sweetness
he hears his name – 'Jamie,
James Forsyth, is my Jamie there?'

She'd tramped across Scotland –
his Lizzie – with a basket and siller
from their kist. A helpful soul
threads a string through the bars.
Then iron-shod heels ring
on the cobbles. 'I'll hae this.
Pit that whig bitch
whar she belongs.' Heavy
with child, she's shoved through the door.

Dunnottar, 1685

'Get on you limmer, you thrawn
auld whoor.' Driven at a pike's end.
Some died in the dust by the wayside
on that forced march from Fife.
Then they found a cart for the old and wasted.
And Lizzie sat in the sun, hands roped
as if she might jump and run.
Now they shamble down the path
to climb into Dunnottar, that battered citadel.

On this May day the peewits crying
over the new-green corn rigs,
gulls and guillemots stacked
along red cliffs – and the sea
like pale blue velvet. Did their iron God
allow for beauty? Would they see it
through the ache of their wounded feet?

Then a door is forced shut on the press.
And ragged voices find their strength:
The Lord hath chastened me sore:
    But he hath not delivered me to death.
Open ye unto me the gates of righteousness,
        That I may go into them,
          and praise the Lord.

Some live that vault in the eye of eternity,
find deliverance, transfigure
Dunnottar's walls to their faith's fortress.

In the Vault

A floor of undressed stones.
No tub for the relief of nature.
They stood, took turns to sit,
envied the bold freedom of the rats.
Some passed, in these summer days,
into their minds' winter.

Folk heard of their plight,
brought food to the guardhouse –
were turned away. Their only
provisions were what they could buy –
the Governor's brother
was a merchant in Stonehaven.

On the Sabbath they'd sing their Psalms,
take up the Precentor's line,
build a wondrous tracery
intricate as the gothic they'd destroy,
till God's light burst
into the chambers of their captive hearts.

Nativity

Born with no stars in your hands –
but speedwell blue,
your eyes.
Good luck for travellers –
and you just passing through?

No sun for this twilight.
Though over the wash
of waves,
soul-haunted gulls, you'd hear
the hint
of a skylark
singing, climbing, singing
as he climbs
till lost in the light.

You brought your gift of flowers
into this dark vault.
You're swaddled in a shawl –
but the wise men
are lost in their theology.

Diary of Lady Athunie
June, 1685

'After her delivery, on the third day,
Mistress Forsyth passes into a fever.
I send a note to the Governor's wife.

She comes, concerned, with a napkin
to her face and two militia
to guard the door. We exchange a look.

On the fourth day, Lizzie falls into a raverie –
red hornygollachs are crawling up the walls.
Mistress Keith brings a pint-stowp of water.

On the fifth day, a morning remission.
Like a March sun, her smiles are cautious.
Then in the evening, a suppression of milk.

On the sixth day the infant falls
into a dwine. In the night, Lizzie's fever
rages. There are palpitations of the abdomen.

On the seventh day, in the morning,
James Forsyth takes joy in the abatement
of her fever. We fear mortification.

The infant sucks on a strip of linen
soaked in cow's milk. Her gums
are dry, her eyes tearless, sunken.

This night red spots and streaks
spread down Lizzie's long bones.
Her face is darkening like a thunder cloud.

On the eighth morning her heart is racing,
her breathing, stertorous. It fills the vault.'

Wordless

How a breath will hover in frost,
pass who knows where, a pebble
sink, and the sea close over,
seamless. She lies in her strangeness –
a house abandoned – ash
in the grate. Forsyth fights his disbelief.
Exposed to that bitter season,
he shakes, stares into the gulf
that has opened at his feet, re-lives
in numb wonder the moments
when their spirits passed. And her life,
robust in love and laughter, fleeting
as the shadow of a bird. Bewildered
by the throng he wonders what to do –
when nothing can be done.
Craves solitude, the long hills,
the infinite sky. And John Fraser
sits by him, mercifully wordless,
a kindly presence, brings water
through the timeless hours. They come
for the corpses. Then someone begins,
'I am the resurrection and the life....'
He hears the door thud shut.

To the Most Honourable, the Marquis of Montrose, Lord President of the Privy Council

My Lord,
We would respectfully draw your attention
to the most grievous sufferings of the prisoners
in the Castle of Dunnottar where men and women
are held promiscuously together and most
barbarously used with so little meat
and drink as scarce keeps us alive.
In our sore travail in these dark vaults
we are visited by prison fever. We petition the council
to give warrant for the governor to allow
friends and servants of the prisoners to bring in
such meat and drink as is necessary
for our sustenance and to allow for the purchase of such
necessities at reasonable rates. We would ask you,
my Lord, for most speedy remedy
of the extreme harshness of our circumstances.

Your humble servants,

Jean Moffat
Marie Gibsone

Mistress Keith Petitions her Husband

The Governor sits at his denner.
He thumps the table, sets
the claret jumping. 'Wheesht,
woman. What in Hell's name
am I to do with eight score Whigs?'

The evil that grows from circumstance –
beyond intention: no
concrete posts, barbed
wire, machine guns, no
trains or cattle trucks
to further efficiency. Just
a green-slimed, barrel vault
five paces south and
twenty paces east
with a rubble floor that might
drain slurry down
towards two narrow windows.

And besides, he was fastidious,
feared nits in his periwig
and the unclean made him gag,
provoked his indignation. He wouldn't see
how degradation and contempt walk
hand in hand, descending
a stair that spirals into darkness.

Concession

Herring gulls rise
and fold on a stack.
Fulmars bank
round the castle rock –
that easy freedom.
Martins flicker
across the gulf.

Four minutes
in the sun and then
no light, no
air – an exchange
of nightmares. For forty
men are taken
to another vault.

Man after man
they lie on their bellies
by a slit in the wall,
suck in the summer.

And fears fly
into their heads
like bats into darkness.

A farmer sits
rocking in his excrement
weeping for his mother.
A boy is babbling

by a wall, his scrabbling
fingers worn
to flesh. John Fraser
of Pitcalzean has been seized
by the bloody flux.

A good man –
in his weakness, he's lost
the Presbyterian bray
that bounced from the implacable
key-stoned roof.

Woman at a Window

Lady Athunie is sitting at a window.
　　As if lost to a dream
　she's watching a doo on the sill, a rippling
　　rainbow scarfing its neck –
that intent ruby eye. She stretches
　　her hand and it lifts, lifts,
into the light of the world's first day.

For Mistress Keith had come again
　　to see the prisoners, discovered
John Fraser in great travail, and had
　　prevailed – 'In the name, Sir,
of Christian charity!' Twelve men
　　were moved from the airless vault
and the women found two rooms.

Testimony of John Fraser

'We twelve have room and air enough.
I'm finding the strength to grope
along the walls. I stop for a breath
by the door thinking of nothing in particular,
head bowed, palms against the timbers,
when, suddenly, I know joy, such
joy as I have never known. My heart
is singing, tears in my eyes, and words
are ringing in my head – *The greatest*
of these is love, the greatest, love.
I seem to walk between the words
as if by soaring, sunlit pillars.
Blinded, I see my God was in my head,
as surely confined as in these vaults –
by anger, indignation, febrile certainties.
God was in my head – and love
had languished. I stand, a prisoner
at a door – and it has opened unto me.'

Escape

A north sea dawn. Stretched
wide overhead, high cloud,
rippling, flowing like a scarlet river
from its source in gold dazzling
on the horizon. And the cliffs incandescent
as if burning in the primal flux.

Twenty five men had climbed
through a window in the great vault
into June's midnight glimmer. Out
on the rock, the timid had clung,
fearing to move – and fell.
Their broken bodies nudge and grate
in the slounging red of the dawn tide.
In the hue and cry fifteen are retaken.

Late in the evening the more-or-less
living are thrown back into the vault.
Their flesh is livid, wealed. Ribs
and arms are broken, hands blistered,
some fingers charred to the bone.
We hold water to their broken mouths.
In the night, Alexander Dalgleish dies.

They'd been tied, in the guard house,
supine, to benches, their arms strapped
under, and burning match-cords held
between each finger. For three hours
militiamen blew to keep them alight.

Mr Fraser Sends Word to the Great Vault

'Your cries for justice must surely be heard.
But heap not coals upon their heads
in the name of God's vengeance. For the spirits
that vaunt His authority are the same
that destroy in its name. They live
in an enchantment of the will. I see it in our own –
the glittering eye, that pounding certitude.
Their God becomes infernal. In His name,
they throw off all constraint
and loving-kindness, take joy in that licence
that lets the beast push free.
And those country loons that lay on the flags
and blew on matches knew something
of that strange exhilaration. They return to their weans,
they kiss their wives but always, behind them
is the shadow, the knowledge they've supped
with the Devil. Haunted by distance they starve
in love's absence, grow cruel
in its pursuit. Brethren, if we have not love
we are as sounding brass. We have no
pillars of fire, no promised land
except our charity. Oh, I know your indignation –
it's loud when I talk with myself,
it would shout me down. But hold not
to their souls the promise of damnation –
rather, proffer salvation in your love.'

The Un-dead

And a few – the un-dead –
are loose in the Mearns. Rising
from ditches they terrify children –
then pass, these haggard ghosts,
like twists of haar under the sun.
Though they'll be remembered
in the winter winds' lamentings.

John White, shepherd, drinks
and washes in the blessed
Water of Bervie. By Fordoun, drops
like a kite on a shirt drying
over a hedge, gorges on eggs
by the Loch of Kinnordie – sets
black-capped gulls frantic.

Tramps the Great Strath
that summer, howks tatties,
scythes hay and barley.
He lives behind the shutters
of his eyes. He'll hurry
his crust to a quiet corner,
eat like a starving dog.

He'll vanish at a question,
appear like the grey bodach
at another bothy door.
He hovers at the edge of thought
like a meaning they've forgotten.
Some see that he's looked
where they'd never dare.

William Hanna of Tunnergarth

Skin shrunk round the skull, thick
hair draggled white, black
beetling eyebrows bridging
the hooked nose – out of their twilight
they hear their prophet from the wilderness:

'Brethren, prepare for the day of salvation
for the Lord will preserve us. He will say,
You that are bound, go forth,
for the Lord will comfort his people.
He will have compassion on the afflicted,
the prey of the malignants will be delivered.
And the Lord will feed our oppressors
with their own flesh, yea, they that contend
with thee shall be drunk of their own blood.
The sheep have been scattered upon the mountain,
and all heaven is affronted.
Mr Fraser would have us read the mind of God,
exhorts us to charity in His name.
But the Lord cries to His ministers,
Vengeance is mine. I will repay.
And all should stand in fear and trembling
before the wrath of His terrible judgement.
He shall blow his trumpet over the mountains
and the children of the Covenant will rise
brandishing swords of retribution, yea
they will flash like lightning over the heads
of the mighty, yea even with the jawbone
of an ass will they slay their thousands.'

Messengers

While gulls raise
their generation
and watch them try
their wings on the wind,
while linties
sing in the whins
and flowers nod
under visiting bees,
Lady Athunie
sits at her window
and Mistress Keith
stands at her side.
They're watching the sky's
messengers – wheeling
pigeons – how they're
lost against
the sun, then turning,
become substantial
on a blue-black cloud.

Lady Athunie's Diary
July, 1685

'Argyle's invasion is over, our story
is abroad, so now the Privy Council
find time to acknowledge our petitions.

The Earls of Errol and Kintore arrive,
braw gallants in their lace and velvet.
They offer the Oath of Abduration.

We refuse to renounce the Covenant.
Their lordships hardly deign to speer
into the stinking vaults. They stand upwind.

How to address this affront to all decency?
The Council directs we be taken to Edinburgh –
fright-white, skeletal, like souls from the Pit.

In Leith, they re-examine us – release
fourteen, the desperately sick and those
who've given a glimmer of satisfaction.

We are banished to America, never
to return on pain of death. I shall pay
my passage, pray for fair winds.

Most will be indentured – gifted to John Scott,
laird of Pitlochy, who hopes, thereby,
to be enriched. He'll charter a ship.

The Council, as councils do, have set
their problem sailing over the horizon.
But they cannot freight contempt.

I can see that moment when ropes
slip from the quay and the ship nudges
into a troubled firth. Then a slow, cold

severance as fields sink into the sea
and the last hilltops growing
insubstantial as a winter breath.

With grieving heart, I leave my country.
My daughter is resolved to go with me
to find freedom in New England.'

Passage

Out into the Atlantic, the *Henry & Francis*
carrying them to Babylon, their bodies' exile.
Through swaying hatches they catch white
sails and rags of blue September.

In the first gale of the equinox they hear
the rigging sing. The sick are moaning
with the ship's companionable groans.
Six hours they heave-to, the bellies
of waves measuring their length, yawing
and pitching in howling spindrift.
Tarpaulins lashed across gratings, they roll
in the 'tween-decks in utter darkness.
Not a day out and the salt-beef
stank. They gnaw at crawling biscuit.

Then west by south on the Canary Current
they arrive on a legendary sea. Unmoving,
held under the eye of the tropical sun
they're exposed to merciless inspection. They might
have seen wonders – but they brought the shadow
from their dark vaults. Day by day
the rose-red rash – they die in delirium.
Stitched in canvas, the grey ghosts
fall, trailing bubbles, down,
down, twisting into endless blue.
Over the shrouds tropicbirds plunge
and dolphins play between lanes of sargassum.

And Lady Athunie walks amongst them,
comforts the dying. Lozenges of sunlight
play under the gratings. A young man
in black, a passenger, sits in the dapple –
he might be reading in a summer wood.
His book catches her eye – the text
is in Latin. He's lost in a song of invention –
James Gregory's design for a reflecting telescope.
She sends him to the Captain.
Under his sceptical command the youth
is unflinching. That night, with the Captain's
glass, they find the moons of Jupiter.
Hunched at the chart table, Thomas
explains a new mathematics. By midnight,
they're discussing Hooke's *Micrographia* –
the youth draws a louse. They find him
a dead man's berth in steerage.

In the small hours, under the swathe
of the Milky Way, the Captain plays
his fiddle on the poop deck. Out
over still waters his music reaches –
passes into something more
than silence. While at his feet sea creatures
trail their own bright galaxies.

James Forsyth

How much loss
can we endure?

He remembers
a morning by the Nith
and a man fishing.
Mayflies sailing
here and there
and trout slapping
in the sun. Irish
troopers are riding by.
They would have the angler
take the test.
They bind his wrists.
At musket point
they drive him up the brae,
stand him against
his barn door.
A volley
crashes
into his head. His wife,
distracted, picks up
pieces in her apron.
They ride off
with three stirks.

Amidst the dying
he wonders why
he lives. Longs
for his final release.
Her breathings reach
out of the night,
her palpable, fevered
hands. And the milky
blue eyes.

They clear the dead
in the mornings. But now,
no seemly
burials. Today
they pushed four
through a port
into the eager ocean.

Storm

George Scott of Pitlochy and his wife,
Lady Athunie, her daughter with her son,
ship's crew.... More than three score die.
And Jeannie Moffat walks between them –
the girl with grey eyes.

And the Captain, his eye on profit from indentures,
sets course for Jamaica. A man
divided – as we are. But the sky
bruises purple, the wind heaves, decks
are awash and the helmsman flung from the wheel.
In the thump and shudder they spring a leak.
Down in the stinking bilge, the carpenter up
to his chest. Hour on exhausting hour
they pump. A chain carries buckets
to the howling deck. As they rig a joury,
three men are swept to their deaths.

Two days and a night they fight
the storm. At midnight, 'tween decks,
Fraser calls through wailing darkness,
Remember Jonas, cast into the sea.
As the waves rolled over him he cried
unto God for deliverance. Even from the bowels
of leviathan God heard his cry. Even
as he was like to faint away, Jonas
looked towards God's holy temple.
But they find little comfort. For the storm

without has conquered within. They strain
through the dark, listening for shifts
in the wind. Then at four in the morning
the gusts became fitful. Ducking through bilge,
the able shift ballast. Inch
by slow inch they pump the slurry,
expose a split between starboard strakes,
tight-drive wedges, caulk and tar.

The wind shifts to the east, stirs
in a few feeble flurries and the pale
dawn flushing as if with the ghost
of a fever. They wake from their nightmare:
Many are the afflictions of the righteous,
but the LORD delivereth him out of them all.

And suddenly it arrives – that love, unbidden.
And Fraser knows the smallness of humanity,
how darkness visits while the rest of the world
still turns. And he thinks of home
and the fields of Pitcalzean, the rye rippling
in an August wind, hears the bell of the kirk
and curlews calling along the winter shore.

Jean Moffat

'My father's house was a temptation.
Comforts of the flesh reached
from his table, wealth whispered
from its tapestried walls. And yet
I knew hunger. Of an afternoon
I'd search his library – on this
he looked kindly – but was never
fed. While my brothers
stravaiged in Edinburgh, I walked
the woods and hills, raised
my eyes to God's glory.

And in His Providence, He led
my feet. I heard His praise
on the wind, followed to the brink
of a corrie. A thousand souls
were standing below me, heads
bowed. And the Word broke
into my heart. I refused the curate,
rejoiced in following that minister
of the moors. 'You catch at shadows,
lassie,' raged my father.
He paid my fines – but the Lord's
countenance had shone upon me.'

Renewal

His fever passed. Forsyth
was denied his wish. Drawn,
ash-pale, eye sockets
bruise-blue – and his mind
struggling to engage. Jean Moffat
had tended him, wondered
at his deliverance.
Fraser would sit by them.

Between glimmers, Forsyth
would fall into the murk
behind his eyes.
Then she'd ask about Lizzie
and try to lead him
through kinder memories.

And in time he told
how she was sitting in a cart
on their way to Dunnottar, the sun
warm on the parks of Strathmore,
the Grampians blue-shimmering
along the horizon.
She'd passed into a doze, bonny,
ripe with the bairn, swaying
as they lumbered
by new-leaved oaks
through light and shade.

And it came to him, so
strangely in their circumstance,
that whatever befell
he would have this moment.

He lay with his eyes tight shut.

'It wasn't what it seemed, John,
it wasn't what it seemed.
What looked like integrity,
an unshakeable faith,
was my heart's arrogance,
a squaring of schoolboys.
And Lizzie and the bairn
have paid the price.'

And in the remembering
he'd carried them
to that far place. Then Jean
and John exchanged glances.
Made their discovery.

19th December, 1685

Smoke-blue, a smudge along
the horizon – a band of cloud?
Then fulmars glide by.
A raft of eiders warps
in the wake. Then a shout
from the main-top. Gently
canting to starboard, three
endless hours and they sail
into a tree-lined bay. White
on black, December trees
are stark, elemental in snow.
There's a hint of wood-smoke
on the breeze.

Swept north, past
Jamestown and Virginia's plantations –
the storm providential – they make
their landfall in Raritan bay.
Perth Amboy is a straggle
of wooden houses by a pier.
To the north east, Statten Island.
And they rise from hell, these
ghastly souls, crowd
the deck, take to the shrouds.

For something has passed away –
what shifts in the human soul,
what knowledge marks its passage

to freedom? That quiet revolution.
'Brethren,' cries Mr Fraser,
'remember the Sabbath to keep it
holy. Let us thank God
for our blessed deliverance.'
Then a psalm builds
from their ragged voices, climbs
into the shivering air:
Sing to the Lord with cheerful voice...
come ye before Him and rejoice.
And Captain Hutton can only
frown: the boatswain survives –
but most of his crew have died.

Then Mr Johnston, Pitlochy's
heir, would have them sign
for four years service.
But they laugh in the cold,
clear air. He stands
in bewilderment, watches
his inheritance pass him by.

Out of my distress, I called
upon the Lord; The Lord answered me
and set me in a large place.
But doors are barred
in this Royalist hamlet. They move
up-country through the snow.

Deliverance

By that snow-bound track
shadows
hovered
between trees
then resolved
into absence.

For half a day they
fought the snow.
Then horses formed
through the flurries,
carried the sick
to a township.
They arrived
by a courthouse
and a deputation –
black-clad, in steeple hats
and bearded.
And by them stood
two tawny boys
in hooded,
wolf fur jackets –
the shadow messengers.

The first of many
kindnesses,
was the burning
of their clothes.

The Deist

'I detest their bigotry.
They ensnare men's souls
with the fear of God, trade
hope for unquestioning
submission, prevail by ignorance
and superstition. Our task is,
step by step, to unfold
the world's wonders
by the new philosophy,
the patient workings of reason.
No spiritual principles
animate nature. The only
authority is reason itself,
the only revelation,
the Divine logos'.

His voice is rising. Forsyth
warns, touches his arm.
'To rule', Thomas whispers,
'by the authority of scripture
is to rule by tyranny.
*Forced worship stinks
in the nostrils of God.*
I took passage to America,
this infant country, in hope
of finding the life worth living,
to help found a polity

on principles of right reason,
where all men and women
are equal and free.'

The young man in black
sets off for Philadelphia.

And Forsyth ponders.

April, 1686

On a south wind
they step into Spring.
John remembers the struggle
to lift his boots
from Scotland's winter clart,
feels the sun's warmth
through the latticed
courthouse windows
and passes
into a haunted,
daytime dreaming – shadows
of gratings
in the groaning 'tween-decks.

The jury returns.

For three months they were free –
then Mr Johnston
claimed his inheritance.
In that oak panelled room,
deep in its solemnity,
in a moment
of stillness,
Fraser is watching his life
as dust motes
dance through sunlight, vanish
in shadow. He catches
Jean's grey eyes –
The Lord is my strength and my song.

Then the judgement:
none had come
of their own accord; none
had bargained for their passage
or signed indentures.
The Governor absolves them.

1st May, 1686

Woodpeckers batter
in a Spring wood.
Rich as butter,
morning sunlight
spills along
green alleys,
scatters
in celandines.
Murmuring with bees,
maples erupt
in a red rash.
New leaves
unfold,
delicate as insect wings.
Across the creek
a shadow flirts
between great pines,
transforms
to a scarlet bird.
Would a black-striped
squirrel
feed from his hand?

And he turns to Jean.
Though undeclared
they know
they will marry.
The sunlight proclaims it
and the woods, loud
with birdsong.

Waterbury, Connecticut

'Do you see the wretchedness
of your condition? Do you believe
that by your own agency you can sanctify
your hearts, avoid God's curse
and wrath? Only by the sunlight
of the Word can you find your way,
yea, even the chief among sinners
can find God's grace.'

Licensed to preach, he wields
his words like swords but walks
benign in his compassion, treads
softly round election and offers
his way to the City of Refuge.
He converts a dozen in their village.

When nightmares stalk behind his eyes,
terror at confinement, racking
storms, he anchors in the calm
of Jean's certainties. She teaches
the few children to read and write.
He works his four acres
by the swine-hog field, helps
build a saw-mill by the waters
of the Roaring River. Folk are wary
of devils in the haunted forest.

A Deputation Visits Sight of the Day
March, 1687

The longhouse is warm. But as he squats
under a haze of wood-smoke, Fraser
sees pinched children's faces.
He'd known the poor starve in Cromarty –
the hind end of winter is cruel.

'Our people pass across the earth
like the seasons and the Great Spirit replenishes
the earth behind them. The white man
settles and spoils. Our young men
are killed or taken, our children die.
The sky is filled with our lamentations.
And you come to buy our land. How can you buy
the sun and wind, the shy deer,
the industrious beaver – the things of the earth?
We are all one spirit. You'd have us follow
your cult of the dead. Lost in your loneliness
you'd have us share your guilt and sorrow.
You talk of a new world but your dreams
of Eden end in a musket shot.'

'But our folk, working their fields,
demand protection. And you know
fine well, in the Fall, a Goodman,
was taken and tortured by fire.'

'And the white-man knows our villages are raided
and captives taken for slavery in Boston.'

Fraser had heard tell of their cruelties.
But it seemed to him that they lived
in the youth of the earth, knew themselves
by hill and forest, animal and bird,
the changing seasons, moved unburdened
by possession, carried no guilt –
eyes wide and free as the land
they lived in. Then he felt the touch
of his vision in the vault – like the gentle shock
of a summer sea – *Love suffereth long,
and is kind*.... And he stretched out his hand.

Song for Watching a Sick Child

Owl wings are brushing the dark.
Through the night silently he comes.
Like a shadow he passes across the great star river.

The spirits are walking the trail of the river.
Owl wings are brushing my child.
Will the owl carry her into the night?

Out of the darkness I see the morning star.
I know the sun will come to us.
It will dance on the ripening corn.

My child will laugh in the sun.
I hear her laughing in the sun.
She will dance with the bees among the flowers.

Parting

They sat on the porch in a warm
darkness, the fireflies here, now
there. The crickets loud.

Forsyth had called by.
The light was returning to his eyes.
'I'm going south, to Maryland.'
Exhausted by his grief, he longed
for a climate that soothed.

'But the Faith, James.
The Faith.'
The moment had grown tense.

'It's not the faith that matters.
It's how we live in it.
They were Christian souls, John.
The Life Guards would have shot me
if they'd had the time.
And Philiphaugh? We slaughtered
women and children. Made
in God's image – are life
and death of so little significance?
Like thrawing a hen in a yard.
And all our large words,
frail against that contempt.'

Their parting was awkward.
In the night that followed
Fraser battled through the hours,
fought the storm of his indignation.
Looked to cockcrow.

Then fell to dreaming.
Saw Sight of the Day standing
by his longhouse – that dignity.
And he woke and knew a truth
in the words of his friend,
felt that calm of arrival
in the haven of the Spirit's mysteries.

He'd watched James pass
into the evening, felt the sadness
of never again. Part of him
went with him. And he
longed to relive that moment –
to redeem his failure of love.

Loss

As twilight slow-swallowed him,
he'd turned and raised his hat.
Rode on. It seemed to her
a severance, so final,
as if all their history
had bidden farewell. As the woods
stepped round them, the phalanx
of the dark, she wept quietly
for her childhood, its loving kindness.

Then she thought of America,
how they stood like children, lost
in its vastness, thought of the savagery
they'd brought – and would surely encounter.
And now she could see how all
peoples were of the earth, partook
of its shape, its nature. She could read
the wilderness in Indian eyes.

They'd carried their own world
from across the ocean, built
palisades to defend it and she
and John had made a life –
but not of their choosing.

Then she saw, as they lived their days,
how loss would grow behind them,
a hinterland of ghosts, autumnal,
bitter sweet, into which life flowed.
And she knew how James would say
what John would fear to think.
But now, in his loss, the voice
she heard was stronger. So that three
would walk together – and be the wiser.

God Bless King William
Summer, 1689

A bloodless revolution. As the news
spread, Boston rioted,
revolt in New York.
They'd fought the Stuarts' taxation –
its manifold injustices – erosions
of freedom. Then Governor Andros
fell with the old order.

Fraser has ridden to Hartford.
As he stands by the Charter Oak –
gnarled, wind-sculpted, wounded –
he thinks how the Word
is established in Connecticut, its folk
invested with authority to govern.
And it comes to him, that the sun
that stands over his head, is the sun
bringing summer to Scotland.

He remembers *Ros an Ear* –
its winter trees spectral
in a layered mist and the sun
hanging, a tarnished coin,
its light suspended
till it breaks in a silver curtain
across the hills. Then the first song
of the thrush – that moment
when Spring speaks from the earth –
and the ewes heavy, expectant.

Glencorse, Scotland, 1694

The wood gripped in a trance
of frost – but the slanting sun
just carried a hint of Spring.
High in an oak, jackdaws
were restive in a globe of light.

They'd seen a roe deer, still,
so still. And watching.
Then it passed like a shadow
between the trees.
And Fraser remembered the wilderness.

'The Indians father. Tell us
about the Indians.' They were sitting
on a great, grey beech.
They'd found it, after a storm,
uprooted in the woods. So
stark, so arbitrary in mortality.

And the dead came into his mind,
that procession of misery
walking the years from Dunnottar,
their grey shapes reaching,
crying out from the pitching dark.

Then out of the moment's night
he felt a surging power,
that exalted fear when his God
would rise, disclose Himself

on the soul's darkness
like a glittering star-path –
the way of the Word to Salvation.

It passed. But now as he looked,
he saw that the trees, the sky,
his children, had been new-made.

And he remembered Forsyth –
and understood his words anew:
their veiled demand to love, to find
a habitation where Word
and charity would dance together.

Did they travel the same road?

And where lay the impulse
that craved purity of doctrine,
that knew no quarter,
that called down the fires of God?

Then he knew his own preaching
had engendered betrayal
of that moment in the vault at Dunnottar.

'Father! Please – the Indians!'
Then he smiled through his anguish
and passed into another time.

Glencorse, 1696

Wings of flame – the windows
framed like fiery angels.
Here and there they licked
through the wooden walls, took
strength, surged and warped
in the buffeting wind. Then the roof
yawned. Sparks soared,
exultant, into the dark, fire
danced on the martyred ribs
of the steeple. Slowly, it folded,
crashed in an ultimate roar.

They watched in awe and wondered
at their final end, felt
the searing breath of the pit.
No figures walked that tumultuous
furnace, no shadowy messengers
stepped free. By the light
of morning they gazed on desolation.
But folk could read the sign.
They'd worked into the dusk,
but the last pew fitted, a joiner
had left a candle burning.

The new church in ashes,
Fraser is called to Alness.
He'd feared he'd lost his language
but as they pass Ben Wyvis,

majestic in snow, take
the road by the crooked firth
serene under the winter sun,
the Gaelic comes unbidden
to his mouth, his childhood cadences.
And word and place and people
resolve into his lost inheritance.

Reflections
Alness, 1711

'Which one are you?' asks the mirror.
That aging face. The same – yet not
the same. Even now, not yet
at ease.

So much you cannot enter –
though you meet them, perhaps, at moments,
on frail bridges of words stretched
above the turbulence. And you weary
of the everyday – harrying backsliders,
the tardy at their catechisms, addressing
diversions that desecrate the Sabbath.

Then you see how you carry your own
vault, become your own prisoner, bound
by the past and that more subtle slavery,
the heart's betrayal of reason, the fall
into temptation. And who, thus bound,
can stand to defy the sway of corrupt and
profligate kings? Freedom begins
and ends in the spirit.

That voice from the pulpit.

How the reaching – that passionate distraction –
the blood and anger – destroyed the grace
you longed for. What, then, is right

action? Is God's purpose our submission?
You think yourself into darkness.

                      Though at times,
of a bright morning, you lift your eyes
and praise. For you know the mystery of two
in one, where what is shared needs
no expression for it's carried quietly
in the bone till it speaks in a scarlet
winter dawn or settles, delicate, flawless
as a snowflake on a sleeve, or sings
through a blackbird or meadow flowers.

And spring – when the young, their blood
raging, fly from your grip? You forget
your own youth – then catch Jean nursing
a secret smile.

            And your love of the land?
A knowing acceptance: its summer-blue
distances drawing the eye wide; then winter –
a dour, reluctant light in the midst
of darkness, its hardness for life and spirit,
age and infancy cut down.

Then you see
how you'd mouthed the husks of words –
suffering and *death* – before you'd tasted
the bitter kernels and tried to walk
your own soul's labyrinth.

And always
this war: your black authority – and loving
kindness; justice – and grace. You live
your days in the knot of contradiction.
You walk by the autumn river and try
to pick yourself free. But at your feet
it mutters and coils in a perpetual weave.

Then who am I?

I catch the dark beauty.
And I know that the river flows to the sea.

In Memoriam Revd. John Fraser
Alness Old Parish Church, April, 2013

There's a wren's song from the ruin,
solemn and strong; the Firth
is boisterous in a sunny wind:
and the past arrives in the palpable
present carrying your name.

'Dangerous Building', say the notices.
I can afford to smile, hoping
your preaching made it so. 'Rantings
of a rebellious schismatic,' did they say?

Then I find your memorial. The legend
is time-blurred, the stone has crumbled,
though a skull and crossed bones
survive. On impulse I bend
to touch the grass over your grave –
then wonder why. It feels like a small
courtesy, like greeting the friend
of a friend after a long journey.

And I rise to something shared –
this vista between the yew trees.

Scribbles

March 17th

A humped leaf.
With stud buttons?

A bronzed fella, dressed
in the lustre of the wet pavement –
and the rush-hour
traffic grey-spraying by.

Have you stopped
to consider, frog?
To your right, wheels crush;
to your left, a bank
of spare, brown hazels.

Even through the murk
they're bright
with yellow-brushstroke catkins
and dabs
of green are unfolding
from tight-packed buds.

Spring driven,
you lurch towards some
assignation
like a running-down
clockwork toy.

Was it you and your siblings
last May on the mud
scattered
like punctuation marks?

Now here you are.
Do I lift
and save you from travelling
this perilous ribbon?
Or trust to the spark
that has lit you so far?

There and Here

In the fields by the Research Station
the sheep are shampooed, weekly.
The Friesians have been recently re-sprayed.

They arrange themselves in tactful,
painterly groups in a radiantly
green landscape.

Here, skulking in a corner,
three elderly tups, bedraggled,
stained as old fire-side rugs.

They chew on ochre stubble.
One holds up a rotting foot in hope
that the rainy wind might sooth.

Upwind, four dry-stane
dykes away, their dreams are grazing.
Something's in the air.

In a hopeful fumble
one mounts a mate. You see
in his eyes the glaze of futility.

For how many Springs,
he worries, can he nurture
the frail smoulder of his lechery?

At Dawyk
For Fran and Habib

Sharp-drawn, new
                beech leaves
glazed
      in a shower. And sunlight
wedged
        through sullen cloud, makes
landfall
        round this tree, ghosts
white,
      grey limbs that
push and
        twist
           for the elusive
light.
      That momentary
assertion, that flash
           of signature,
shouts
      from its own detritus.
                Beyond
that magic circle,
        bluebells
in the painted grass
         ring
at the song of a thrush,
           its patient,
sharp insistence
        honed

on the steel of flashing rain.
We scan
      the patched hills,
plot
   the skirmishing light
and water,
     happy at our encounter
in something
      shared.

Seed
For Emily

You bounce. And that
itch in your skipping feet
is infectious. I weigh
the temptation, look furtively
round the Garden Centre
to see who would see.

We're buying plants
and seeds for her garden –
her seventh birthday.

It's not something we
remember – when we last
skipped. And the witnesses
lost. That vertigo –
stepping into a country,
that only I can people.

Light as a bird. And now
you're all childhood
dancing there. And the packets
in your hand charged
in a way you cannot know.

Wasps

Loud in a May boom, this hedge,
with wasps in black-and-gold
bikers' leathers, elegant in their ferocity.
And in their faded hand-me-downs,
hover flies, search-and-rescuing
deep into the pink of cotoneaster flowers.

Bees like furry ginger finger-ends
dig and delve. And on the picnic rug
you're half-way through an apple.
There's a crust on your plate. All intent –
that universal appetite. And Spring leaves
drawing their surge from the root.

Then you dance, dance, arms flailing.
'Wasps! Wasps!' 'Stay still.
They won't harm you.' The forced
adult calm is hardly persuasive
for the boom, is filling your ears –
the wasp-strain piercing. Retreat.

Come winter we'll look for the wasp-town,
find it, perhaps, in the hedge,
grey and tattering in the wind.
That paper miracle. But somewhere
that we'll never find, like something
in a fairy tale, will lie a sleeping Queen.

Yesterday

Half asleep – and memory
stirring with yesterday's echoes.

A sunlit reach of water
is a mirror polished by rain.
Beneath the illusion of surfaces
birch and willow search
into depths, their Gothic traceries
and dark green leaves
more vivid than the life.

A cloud passes. Their mystery
concedes substantiality
to wood and leaf and rock.

Do you remember when we
were more vivid than the life?

By Aberfoyle

A cascade through the roof of a wood
soothes to a honey-brown pool.
It reflects a snow-and-sun
patched bank where knuckled
trees grip at the declivity –
Waterfall of the Little Fawn.

Slowly, towards it, walks
a girl with a white cloche hat
like the calyx of a Spring flower.
She's dabbing her eyes with a tissue.
She might be your daughter.
A boy, by her side, observes her
from the corner of his eye.

March – no hints of green
except for the open weave
of moss and sombre filigree
of lichen. She hardly sees
the waterfall. Can she hear
beyond the roar in her ears?
Unreachable, that unhappiness.

Held at your near distance
you watch the burn's turbulence
resolve to a fawn in a mirror.
And will them to see.

Under the Weather
For Charlotte

Under the weather, I hear.
And imagine a ship rolling,
pitching, punching into lifting
seas, and a whimpering rag
dank in a gloomy corner.

But here you are, just a wee
bit pasty and your summer-sky
eyes still bright. And you're busy
at your colouring book making
a path for a breezy butterfly.

It jiggles and squiggles along
a page, moving in joy
across black-drawn outlines
of animals – become cages. And how
odd this exotic menagerie.

Have you ever met a giraffe?
I roar in sympathy as you cross
a lion – but doubt you've encountered
a mouse in your pristine house.
Let alone scribbled on it.

By the Water of Leith

The rock ice-scoured,
a secret beneath the city's
calculating eyes,
a thread of connection
to a grey firth
from Autumn hills patched
in purple September.

A heron is lost
in a green mirror.
Then back and forth –
an agitation. It cuts
the air like a child
with scissors. Zig-
zag, up and down.

You see by the reflection
a bridge has opened its
eye in surprise.
Then you catch in slants
of sunlight, gnats,
like stardust. And the air
thick with their glitter.

There's a bloke with a sandwich
leaning against a rail.
'Bat!' we say – and smile
in recognition – skin
strung on the veins
of a last year's leaf.
Our noon – their midnight?

Blizzard

Raw as a wound, dawn
opens between the Moorfoot Hills
and snow-heavy cloud.
Sun-dazzle floats its orange
stain, effortless, over drifts
that might be non-negotiable.

I stamp into the porch, hear you
busy in the kitchen listening
to Mozart while you ice
the Christmas cake. We meet
there, in that beauty – crystal
sharp. A countess sings for us.

Outside, sugar lies
two feet deep,
locks us into private worlds.
Nothing can be heard beyond
that singing cold. Except
the silence that fell with the snow.

Christmas Week
For Alice and Robbie

Scribbles – after they've left sometimes
we find them. Dark red
on a midnight-blue chair, orange
on polished mahogany – their colour sense
can be subtle. They could be mind-maps
of their day – intense, passionate, crossed
threads of wailing purposes. Suggestive
as ciphers, they defy translation.

I remember, 'thou shalt not,' and prickly
horsehair chairs where I fell
into the evil trance of boredom. Even
raised from the pit for the Sunday walk,
sepia prison shades stained
the sunniest day. Perhaps, even now,
they insinuate into Sunday shadows –
a sense of something missed in the passing.

It's not that children want to make
their marks – nothing so trivial. More,
fascination with a process. And if its untranslatable
it signifies, for us, a house a little
worn in the wearing, like a comfortable shoe –
no prickly chairs, screw clamps
of tedium – a place, not merely
happy, but like old Christmases, merry.

West and East

By Trosaraidh
April

Exhausted, it seems, this landscape.
Across Eiseaval's shoulders, the heather
is rain-dark, winter scorched. Reeds
over the peat-lands are straw-brown
patched with distant rumours of green,
the lochans steely. Humped, barnacled,
wet gneiss gleams, its boulders
strewn like stranded cetaceans.

Driven on a north wind,
slanting showers lead blue-black
clouds along the Atlantic horizon.

By the road we walk, in the shelter
of a ditch, a sudden sun distils a bank
of primroses, sets kingcups glittering
in the seep of peat-brown puddles.
And in a corner of a croft, surprised
as it will ever be, a lamb drops
from warm darkness, into the bitter light.

By Tigh a Rubha

The red house on the point
has been breached by winter storms.
Seven ravens lift
through a gape in the roof.
Black silk and tatters,
ungainly as widows in a high wind,
they flump across the tiles,
jostle for a chimney.
Quaark. Quaark. They launch
and write their poetry on the air.

Their free lunch lies
headless in the rubble of a room.
The fleece has sunk like old thatch
through the rafters of the ribs.
Somehow the skull has crept
through the door and died
in the bracken by a peat stack.
Red tiles and lost purposes
are scattered through the buttercups.
Intruders, we shift away.

What croaked ceilidhs unfold
along the rafters under
that broken roof? I expect,
like us, they endlessly discuss
the weather, study the slabs
of sun or moonlight, the slant
of rain, natter about spells
and the passing of old wisdom.
Quaark. Quaark. They're back.
Dropping through the roof.

For Effie

To say, *never again,* is to set you
drifting behind in the turbulence,
something cast off that the sea
swallows, something that might
never have been. But this loss
is more – and less – than absence.
For we remember fondly.

Paused at your threshold we said,
Goodbye, Look after yourself,
See you next summer, and I caught
from under your breath – *If*
we meet again. Then you tilted
your head, the way birds do,
and smiled. And I wondered –
the wise caution of age
or whispers from the bone? As if
you wanted us to hear and
not hear. Your words stayed
with me – a stain on the day.

As we stood at the rail sailing
from Lochboisdale, the usual tug of loss
seemed more an evisceration.
We passed into a grey sky
fallen on a fractious sea,
all marks shrouded.

We return to a waking land
and something bequeathed: a richer
meaning in the nerveless world –
sand and the moods of water,
indifferent birds, the ruthless
beauty of Spring flowers,
these ancient hills – as if,
in our remembering, we find you
in the place you loved.

And every wave a folding over,
till that searching rush at landfall
and a momentary glitter.

At Balranald

We pass under the shadow of a raven.
  Then an edge of cloud cuts
the machair. Cold rain strikes.
  We shelter behind a dune.
Insubstantial as a ghost, the rock
  of St Kilda has come and gone.
The rain shroud shifts. We watch
  its grey mood pass
along the Uist hills. Now blue,
  deepest blue, the Atlantic
breaks over rocks at Aird an Runair.
  Lost in that sapphire, I wake
to a question – can a wave be fathomless?
  That endless climb – to a pause,
to a slow fold down the face
  of its mineral light. It shatters,
seethes in blue-veined, glittering white.

  A crèche of eiders lifts
and falls in the lee of a sill. Imagine –
  knowing no before or after,
adrift on the winter ocean, lost
  in the heave of the perpetual moment.

At Kilaulay

Waves are beating
at the door of my waking,
the wind is fevered
and the blind sun
squandering in rain.

We are adrift,
my love, all's sheered
away that makes
a homecoming of the morning.

Then I reach
and find myself moored
by the rope of your hand.
And out
of this penitential season
arrives a quiet joy.

At Loch Eynort

Set free, it seemed, from out of the earth,
russet as the moor's winter mantle.
Over the loch it climbed, easy
as a thought, then rode, wings
elbowed, down the wind. And the blue
cut with a diamond round the ridges
of Ben Mhore. It turned, lifted,
spiralled over our heads, till we
staggered, dizzy, clutched at a rock.

Bored by this inspection, it drifted
past the ghost of an afternoon moon
then knowing itself kin to the sun,
soared into its dazzle – and was gone.
Aquila of the tawny eye – had your wax
melted? No drifting feathers
sidling down the light. And I remembered
Heraclitus – how sparks
from the fire to the fire return.

Bogle
For John Brown

Arms wide, a bogle leans
on the wind – draws the bleak machair
into his domain. Wet-black,
his rags have resolved from salt
Atlantic murk. Heavily
they flap – he might be trying to fly.

But who does he fool? A flock
of rock doves curves
over his head; buntings
are fluttering in the bending oats.
Who bothers to acknowledge
such posturing irrelevance?

But he works in us – adds
chill to the drizzle. Unsettling,
that tortured stance, that vain
illusion of striding intention.
For he's stuck in the grip of the earth,
tied to crossed sticks.

He watches his soul's companion,
a ragged buzzard, lurch
across the wind. He envies
the presence that can disturb
a flock of lapwings. It settles
like a savage totem on a post.

On a theme from Dvořák's 'Cypresses'
At Garrynamonie

You call for me to come. The cold
is a shock, and the sun an hour
sunk. Flushed pearl
of the gloaming along the Atlantic rises
to the blue of precious porcelain,
to ultramarine. And the depth –
the depth is endless.

The moon is cut perfectly,
its gold seemingly translucent.
Even the north wind
is struck dumb.

But this night makes demands –
oh, it demands. For its onset
brings a dawning – your shape
cut on lapis, your darkness
lustrous as the pollen-gold moon.
But I can say nothing –
for only nothing seems
eloquent enough.

And I think how far
you are, lost in the reach
of that sky – how near.

Then a theme sings from under the wind.
Where has it slept in the old
labyrinth awaiting this moment?
It wakes to the moon and a night
I can feel on my finger tips.

We return to warmth, shut out
the night. And the moment gone by
like a rinsing wave.

But what of the song
that only I could hear? It sings
of the faith that things
can speak for us – wind and sea,
the golden moon and the light
that is passing to darkness.

From Eriskay

The Sound worried, the wind wondering
if it might stretch to a gale and a gannet working
along breaking seas. White to white,
it plunges in turbulent consummation.

And Atlantic rain in its own waves
scouring grey rocks, releasing
the pink of feldspar, the glitter of quartz –
shades of that deeper, primordial drama.

It rinses the yellow of buttercups, runs
pink ragged robin ragged, bends
blades of irises, batters at a bus
edging along the tentative causeway.

Then rumours of light – as if a switch
had brought white houses to a subtle
incandescence, set hints of emerald
glimmering under swathes of the bay.

The wind is losing its memory. Head-high,
swallows scythe by. A wheatear flutters
from a knoll, twists at a fawn moth.
A blind rolls up along the horizon.

North Sea

This is the sea where night gathers –
where thin-lipped, winter dawns
mouth cold beginnings, where short,
thrawn waves are Sunday-suited,
grey even under the summer sun.
Its seascapes shaped minds that praised
a jealous God. Even its serenities
are deceptions, summon the haars that drew
the dragon ships, their bear-sarks
howling out of the chill. So why
does it lift the heart, disclose
in its turbulence a spirit's haven? I remember
horizons wider than the edge of rain,
the sea inscrolled in parables of light.

After the Storm

A bright green net, blue nylon
twine, a woman's shoe, a battered
lobster pot in stinking tangle
that turnstones tentatively explore,
polystyrene, plastic boxes,
a lamb's skull – meagre in their hints,
the reluctant tides. And over them,
lifts a curlew – that echoing song,
spirit of the sea's edge.

So lives were knitted in dark blue,
not the blue of summer sky
or sea but a fathomless winter dark
under the beacon of a drifting moon.
Spine of the herring, plaited cable –
and God's diamond eye set
in the family runes of a gansey.
Did they believe that love could
prevail over that fearful scrutiny?

Some found His judgement
non-negotiable – a snarling wrath
from the north, a dizzy hull
pitched fifty feet. You hear
a dialogue, calm, assured. A reply
to the coastguard's query stops
mid-sentence…. Again and again
he plumbs that silence, never so intense –
the only answer to his question.

Mauled – limbs and features lost.
But they read the gansey, win
something back – a time to grieve,
relief from what a mother, otherwise,
could never believe. The stound
in the night at footsteps by the door,
at a face fleeting across a window, at the tilt
of a head in a crowd, at depths calling
in a storm – resolved in the knowing.

Passacaglia – St Monan's Church
After Benjamin Britten's Third Quartet

In this ancient shelter, wedged
between earth and punishing sky,
we hear your questions rising
sustained by your bleak honesty –
but, unresolved, they fall
in arches like these gothic windows.
You refuse to drowse into the far
night-reaches of the soul,
so your darkness is burnished,
glimmers with a rumour of stars.

Tick and tock, tick and
tock – and these stones, gesturing
at eternity, merely confirm
our entrapment. Round and round
the hands pass, measure
our slow march round and
round – dignified but harried
by that final silence. Your last
notes climb to its frontier.
We carry their echoes into the weather.

And the sea in agitation, rising,
falling, worrying at the rock –
its stubs and pinnacles stubborn
in their delusion of permanence.
A solitary gannet, a gleam

of pure intention, hurries through
the reluctant light between sea
and charged cloud. Thunder
cracks over the church. Bars
of cold rain begin to fall.

Nightfall

Thrum of heavy engines.
Lights glide across the calm,
dip in the opening swell.
A ship has crossed the bar.
The slow wash unrolls,
curdles along the flats, lapses
into sand. A twilight chill.

Emptiness. A boy hurries
home on the trickle of a path
by the linties' nests. Something
screams in the dunes – tight
in the stoat-jaws? And again.
He feels its night fold in
as buttressing senses fail.

Silence builds on silence,
lets loose a skein
of dreams. Whins quicken,
loom sharp in a child's
panic, dusk bars
whatever way. Feet
sink in mining dream-sand.

Breathless, the sky opens
on a sweep of wet strand.
He follows the map of the tide's
edge to the burn. Listens
for the slap of sea-trout, finds
a glimmer of meadow sweet
that lights the way home.

Weather-eye

As the tide ebbs the wrack settles
never so wet in the sea as plastered
and glistening over black rocks. It leaves
its memory in pools where light shivers
into fry that dart and nudge
into invisibility, where pink shells gleam,
delicate as finger nails. And the child's mind
lost in the quiet under wind and wave.

So the sea becomes the mark for all
experience: brings confirmation of the day
in racketing gulls; creates the weather-eye
drawn to whatever horizon. I dream
in school of wading sun-warmed
shallows, starting as the sand boils
in the wake of a flounder. Gannets dive
down the margins of my jotters.

And what remains is the habit of search
for bird or flower, the scan of loch
or river, the trawl through page
or gallery for that swirl of contact –
the turning fish, the electric pulse
of connection – for the sudden arrival
at something lost: the dolphin child
and his easy shift between realities.

Nor'easter

A call from the sea arrived –
or was it from the blood? – drew me
down deserted wind-bashed
streets, past shivery puddles
and a dark-stained, sailing spire.

Arms flung wide, leaning
on the wind, I watched waves
burst over the sea wall, licked
trickling salt from my face.
Danger was excitement, like something
from the night scarcely contained
by trembling windows.

Holding his hat, a man sidled
from the footbridge at the station.
I resented his intrusion.
He bowed before my storm, harried
to stumbling. Spray rattled at a door
along the street. I conjured it
wide to swallow him.

Next morning, I climbed
strange contours on the beach,
found a drowned cat in the shingle,
the nap of its fur rubbed bald
in startling patches. Gulls wheeled
and mewed like cat-souls over the ebb,
dipped to inspect a sky burial.

I turned for town. Streets
echoed as the dying wind
carried their cries from the sea.

The Joiner

A week afterwards I visited the place.
In auld Davie Bain's but'n'ben
my uncle had made a workshop
where I learned whatever of his craft
I'd ever know from mimicking his gestures:
the sweep of a wooden plane as it flayed
in resinous coilings, the confident
thump at the well-driven nail.

The broken, pink plaster
was a Leonardo notebook where he sketched his plans,
their lines unerring. Stacked across open rafters,
his timber gleamed in winter firelight –
a ceiling where, in summer, nesting sparrows
scuffed. Across his knee he'd thraw the necks
of plump red hens in flurries
of buffeting wings. I'd watch the dead, red eyes
as the limp heads swung. A final
spasm, and he'd tear away the easy feathers.

An expert whistler, he'd perfected
a sort of pibroch on windy planks
while roofing houses, his repertoire, bravura
variations on the auld sangs. He'd soar,
even above the screeching saw.

In his modest way he dealt in resurrection.
With battens from the dump he framed his sheds,
clad them in the tongue-and-groove
of rescued flooring, built aviaries
where spring song rang across the evenings.

Now, with children of my own, I see
his patience. He'd slip me a half-crown
as his apprentice. I began to make a fly-box,
a sort of testimony. As I laboured, grief
grew in my throat like a bitter winter virus.

At Auchmithie

Gulls on this wind are nonchalant.
In a gesture at serenity, blue-grey,
mother-of-pearl, the sky is upturned
mussel shell gleaming above cloud-scud
driven from the east. And the seas
beyond the harbour bar, climbing,
steepling, combing above us as we watch
agile at the tide line. Unsettling,
that tumbling weight of water. Its thunder
echoes under gnawed red cliffs.

You wonder how they rode that turmoil,
passed to homecoming under the walls'
cascades. Pipits are blown like litter
from spindrift-shining rocks; a stonechat
fronts the wind's jostle. Abandoned
on the shingle are four blue cobles –
and the 'Rosebud', some heart's token,
holed. You see beneath stove
strakes its lobster creels, stowed
for another day that never came.

At St Cyrus

Like old dishwater you say – the sea.
I know what you mean – certainly cold
and blue-grey with a froth of tired
bubbles. A few gulls mooch
along the tide's edge, brash
adolescents mottled in muddy brown.

Across a steel sky, chevrons of geese
trail a litter of gabble. Scoters
are working the slack beyond the waves. They flip,
drop, black, into the murk. A wagtail
flickers across the sands. The moody wind
makes clean cuts to the bone.

You frown and huddle. But it makes me
smile – this cussedness. Uncompromising,
no fiddling ambiguities. Come on
you old devil, do your worst. The concrete
plinth of somebody's porch hangs
over a scar where the cliff has fallen.

From walrus ivory, the whalers carved
scrimshaws, the norsemen, pieces for chess.
Here, battering seas have cut stacks
and a sculpture that addresses the sky
like imploring arms. But I'm laughing
in the wind, savouring a bitter freedom.

I think the North Sea is my father.

Sea Music

This vast, sea-stretched
andante, breaks white
against red rock. Grey-green
as winter cliff-grass, tongues
search the sculpted sandstone,
the dizzying, quarried inlets,
where gulls are set in cathedral
niches to catch the frail
warmth of a February sun.
It seems their brethren
cry and wheel
round the echoes of a loss.

And our loss quickens
after the hints – *The Deil's Heid,
The Mermaid's Kirk* – that point
beyond stone and water.
As if folk had found names
for their shadows, or had heard,
within that great symphonic
seascape, strands of song
from mermaids wise
to the price of human love.
We lack the treasure of credulity
that buys the spirit in.

West Ferry

With music in my fingers I walked
the beach. A winter's night,
the moon-froth glittering, sidling
over pebbles, a confluence of light
and air and water on the land's lip –
with the hiss of sleepy breathing.

I'd come across the Nocturnes
in a pile of hand-me-down music.
Can a life change at a note?
I was twelve. I stepped
into the garden of these searching, dark
sonorities and could not leave.

Someone's great aunt had died –
and I wonder, when this dusty maiden
played, if she passed into night
and moon and sea and a girl
wandering. Or sang her stranded
love, the flotsam of war.

When I can, I return to that shore,
for there began that long
accommodation of what we are
to what we find, and how the one
grows with the other – if we can bring,
whatever is disclosed, to song.